THE TEN COMMANDMENTS

THE TEN COMMANDMENTS

STILL THE BEST MORAL CODE

DENNIS PRAGER

REGNERY
PUBLISHING
A Division of Salem Media Group

Regnery® is a registered trademark of Salem Communications Holding Corporation

Library of Congress Control Number: 2015933006

ISBN 978-1-62157-417-0

Published in the United States by
Regnery Publishing
A Division of Salem Media Group
300 New Jersey Ave NW
Washington, DC 20001
www.Regnery.com

Manufactured in the United States of America

10 9 8 7 6 5 4 3 2

Books are available in quantity for promotional or premium use. For information on discounts and terms, please visit our website: www. Regnery.com.

Distributed to the trade by
Perseus Distribution
250 West 57th Street
New York, NY 10107

To my lifelong friend and teacher,
Joseph Telushkin

"Make for yourself a teacher, and acquire
for yourself a friend."

—The Talmud

CONTENTS

FOREWORD

The history of the human race has not been morally impressive.

Slavery was nearly universal. Women, when not enslaved, had few rights. And while progress has been made on both fronts—slavery has been largely extinguished and in some societies women are treated as the equals of men—murder, robbery, rape, and a hundred other crimes, not to mention monstrous horrors such as genocide, continue to this day. Indeed the twentieth century was perhaps the bloodiest century in recorded history. Cruelty has been so widespread in history that it can almost be considered the human norm.

Clearly human nature, while not evil, is not primarily predisposed to goodness. And it is certainly morally weak. When confronted with temptation to do what's wrong, temptation often overpowers conscience.

It would seem obvious, then, that having people do the right thing ought to be the single most important question preoccupying every society and every religious and secular ideology.

But it usually isn't.

Societies are preoccupied with just about everything other than making good people.

For some, it is intelligence. Parents are often more concerned with their children's IQs than their children's characters. And many people confuse higher education with decency and moral insight.

For others, the primary social concern is "face." This has characterized many Asian and Arab societies; hence, such things as "honor" killings.

Or it might be physical beauty, as in ancient Greece, or building an empire as in ancient Rome and nineteenth century Europe.

Or perhaps theology. People have too often valued "proper" religious beliefs more than proper moral behavior, and even slaughtered others for not having the right religious beliefs. This is a common occurrence even in our time.

It might be nature. For such people, it is deemed better to ban rice that has been genetically modified to include vitamin A, and allow a million East Asian children to go blind from vitamin A deficiency than to tinker with nature, thereby potentially harming the environment. Likewise those preoccupied with the natural environment deemed it preferable to ban the pesticide DDT despite the fact that such a ban directly led to the death of millions of Africans to malaria.

And, of course, innumerable individuals are preoccupied with wealth or power.

To repeat, preoccupation with morality—how people treat other people—has been rare.

There was an exception.

The Ten Commandments are preoccupied with goodness. Each commandment is a moral tour de force. Together they present the most compelling plan ever devised for a better life and good world. Yet, they were written—and in the eyes of hundreds of millions, revealed by the Creator—three thousand years ago. The

Ten Commandments are what began humanity's long, arduous journey toward moral progress.

With all our sophistication, the remarkable fact is that the Ten Commandments are more or less all we need. That is what I endeavor to explain here. If you want to improve your life and make a better world, here is the blueprint. The understanding of human nature that you will find in the Commandments is startling in its depth and sophistication. And most important, the Ten remain as germane today as they were to our ancient ancestors.

If people lived by these Commandments, little else would be needed to make a world in which armies spent their time playing football; police would rarely be needed; the doors to our homes could be left unlocked; and women would walk anywhere at any time of day or night without fear of being sexually assaulted. Political corruption would vanish; courts of law would be trustworthy. Strained relationships between parents and adult children would be mollified.

This Prager University book and the corresponding video courses are the culmination of forty-five years of study and teaching. These projects, consisting of eleven parts—an analysis of each commandment plus an introduction—represent a great deal of hard work. I cannot sufficiently thank the many people who made these unique products possible: the editors, the producers, the makeup and lighting people, the brilliant artists, and, most especially, my wife Susan Prager who edited every text, and Allen Estrin, who also edited every text and supervised every phase of production. Prager University is his brainchild.

I hope you enjoy this book, and that it touches your life in a deep way. If so, please consider watching the video courses and know that there are scores—soon hundreds—

of other video courses on almost every subject at www. prageruniversity.com. We release a new course weekly.

We live in a world filled with evil and moral confusion. There is only one way out: affirmation of a God Whose primary demand of us is that we treat our fellow human beings decently. Faith in any god who makes any other primary demand will ultimately fail to solve the problem of evil. And any moral system that is detached from God, no matter how noble and sincerely held, will likewise fail.

That's why the Ten Commandments are the most important thing ever written. They inextricably link God and goodness, making it clear beyond doubt that God Himself is preoccupied with goodness.

And if that is so, what else matters?

Dennis Prager

January 2015

THE TEN COMMANDMENTS

STILL THE BEST MORAL CODE

No document in world history so changed the world for the better as did the Ten Commandments. Western civilization—the civilization that developed universal human rights, created women's equality, ended slavery, created parliamentary democracy among other unique achievements—would not have developed without them. As you will see when each of the Ten Commandments is explained, these commandments are as relevant today as when they were given over three thousand years ago. In fact, they're so relevant that the Ten Commandments are all that is necessary to make a good world, a world free of tyranny and cruelty.

Imagine for a moment a world in which there was no murder or theft. In such a world, there would be no need for armies, or police, or weapons. Men and women and children could walk anywhere, at any time of day or night, without any fear of being killed or robbed. Imagine further a world in which no one coveted what belonged to their neighbor; a world in which children honored their mother and father and the family unit thrived; a world in which people obeyed the injunction not to lie. The recipe for a good world is all there—in these ten sublime commandments.

But there is a catch. The Ten Commandments are predicated on the belief that they were given by an Authority higher than any man, any king, or any government. That's why the sentence preceding the Ten Commandments asserts the following: "God spoke all these words."

You see, if the Ten Commandments, as great as they are, were given by any human authority, then any person could say: "Who is this man Moses, who is this king or queen, who is this government to tell me how I should behave? Okay, so why is God indispensable to the Ten Commandments? Because, to put it as directly as possible, if it isn't God who declares murder wrong, murder isn't wrong. Yes, this strikes many people today as incomprehensible, even absurd. Many of you are thinking, "Is this guy saying you can't be a good person if you don't believe in God?"

Let me respond as clearly as possible: I am not saying that. Of course there are good people who don't believe in God, just as there are bad people who do. And many of you are also thinking, "I believe murder is wrong. I don't need God to tell me." Now that response is only half true. I have no doubt that if you're an atheist and you say you believe murder is wrong, you believe murder is wrong. But, forgive me, you do need God to tell you. We all need God to tell us. You see, even if you figured out murder is wrong on your own, without God and the Ten Commandments, how do you *know* it's wrong? Not *believe* it's wrong, I mean *know* it's wrong? The fact is that you can't. Because without God, right and wrong are just personal beliefs. Personal opinions.

I think shoplifting is okay, you don't. Unless there is a God, all morality is just opinion and belief. And virtually every atheist philosopher has acknowledged this.

Another problem with the view that you don't need God to believe that murder is wrong is that a lot of people haven't shared your view. And you don't have to go back very far in history to prove this. In the twentieth century millions of people in Communist societies and under Nazism killed about one hundred million people—and that doesn't count a single soldier killed in war.

So, don't get too confident about people's ability to figure out right from wrong without a Higher Authority. It's all too easy to be swayed by a government or a demagogue or an ideology or to rationalize that the wrong you are doing isn't really wrong. And even if you do

figure out what is right and wrong, God is still necessary. People who know the difference between right and
wrong do the wrong thing all the time. You know why?
Because they can. They can because they think no one
is watching. But if you recognize that God is the source
of moral law, you believe that He is always watching.

So, even if you're an atheist, you would want people
to live by the moral laws of the Ten Commandments.
And even an atheist has to admit that the more people
who believe God gave them—and therefore they are not
just opinion—the better the world would be.

In three thousand years no one has ever come up
with a better system than the God-based Ten Commandments for making a better world. And no one ever
will.

COMMANDMENT

I AM THE
LORD YOUR
GOD

GOD WANTS US TO BE FREE

What is the first of the Ten Commandments? It might seem like an odd question, but it's not. Jews and Christians give different answers. The reason is that what we know as "The Ten Commandments" is, in the original Hebrew, "The Ten Statements," *aseret ha'dibrot* (עשרת הדברות). And since the Hebrew is the original, we begin with the first statement, which all religions agree, is: "I am the Lord your God who took you out of the land of Egypt, out of the house of bondage." This statement is so important that none of the other commandments make sense without it.

First, it asserts that God is giving these commandments. Not Moses and not any other human being. Second, God is the One Who delivered you from slavery. Again, no human being did this, not even Moses. Therefore you have an obligation to Me, God. And what is that obligation? That you live by the following nine commandments.

This is the beginning of what is known as ethical monotheism, the greatest world-changing innovation of the Hebrew Bible. It means two things. Ethical monotheism means that the one God—that's monotheism—is the source of ethics, of morality. Morality, an objective code of right and wrong, does not emanate from human opinion; it emanates from God, and therefore transcends human opinion. The other meaning of ethical monotheism is that what God most wants from us is that we treat other human beings morally. None of the Ten Commandments concern what humans must do "for" God; pre–Ten Commandments religions all believed that people must do a lot "for" their gods—for example, feed them and even sacrifice people to them.

But now, thanks to the Ten Commandments, mankind learned that what God wants is that we be good to our fellow human beings. Even the commandments concerning not having false gods and not carrying God's name in vain are ultimately about morality. The thing we can do "for" God is to treat all His other children decently. Every parent can relate to this. Parents—or at least healthy parents— have indescribable joy when they see their children act lovingly toward one another and indescribable pain when they see their children hurt one another. So, too, God, Who is likened to our father in heaven, cares most about how we treat other human beings, all of whom are His children.

The third critical teaching of the First Statement—"I am the Lord your God who took you out of Egypt, out of the house of bondage"—is the importance, and the meaning, of freedom.

Note that God is not saying in this introduction to the Ten Commandments that He created the world. It surely would have made a lot of sense for God to introduce the Ten Commandments with the statement, "I am the Lord your God who created the world." That is, after all, pretty impressive, and would make sense: "I created the world: You'd better listen to Me." But no, the one thing God declares is that He took the Children of Israel out of slavery and into freedom. That's how much God hates slavery and how important God considers freedom. The Founders of America based their entire view of America on this belief—that God wants us to be free. That is why the most iconic symbol of the American Revolution, the Liberty Bell, has only one sentence inscribed on it—a verse from the Hebrew Bible: "Proclaim LIBERTY throughout all the Land unto all the Inhabitants thereof."

But there is one other equally important lesson about freedom imparted by the opening statement of the Ten Commandments: what freedom means. The Giver of the Ten Commandments is, in effect, saying: "I took you out of slavery and into freedom, and these Ten Commandments are the way to make a free society. You cannot be a free people if you do whatever you want." Freedom comes from moral self-control. There is no other way to achieve it.

And fourth and finally, by telling us that He liberated the Hebrew slaves, God made clear that He cares deeply about human beings. It is impressive to create the world. But what most matters is not only that there is a Creator, but that the Creator cares about His creation.

All of that is in the one statement with which the Ten Commandments begin.

STUDY QUESTIONS

1. Explain in your own words what the First Commandment means.

2. How do Jews and Christians differ on the numbering of the Ten Commandments?

3. What was so world changing about the Ten Commandments?

4. What do the Ten Commandments say humans must "do" for God? How does that differ from pre–Ten Commandments religions?

5. How does the First Commandment teach the importance and meaning of freedom?

COMMANDMENT

NO OTHER
GODS

THERE ARE MORE IDOLS THAN EVER

L et's discuss the Second Commandment according to the oldest, that is the Jewish, enumeration of the Ten Commandments. In Christian tradition it is the First Commandment. The most common translation begins: "You shall have no other gods before me." The commandment then goes on to prohibit both making idols and worshiping idols.

Most people, when they think of this commandment, understandably think that it only prohibits the worship of idols and the worship of gods such as the ancient pagan gods of rain, of fertility, all the other nature gods and chief gods such as the Roman Jupiter and the Greek Zeus. However, there is a major problem with this understanding of the commandment. Since no one today worships these gods, let alone worships idols made of stone, most people think that this commandment is irrelevant to modern life. The irony, however, is that this commandment is not only relevant to modern life, it is in many ways the mother of all the other commandments.

Why is it so relevant today? Because today we have as many false gods as the ancients did. And why is it the mother of all the other commandments? Because if we identify false gods and avoid worshiping them, we will eliminate one of the greatest barriers to a good world—false gods. So, let's begin by defining a false god. The point of biblical monotheism is that there is only one God and that only this God, the Creator of the universe Who demands that we keep these Ten Commandments, is to be worshiped. Why? First, because one God means one human race. Only if we all have the same Creator, or Father, as it were, are we all brothers and sisters. Second, having the same parent also means that no person or group is intrinsically more valuable than any other. And third, one God means one moral standard for all people. If God declares murder wrong, it is wrong for everyone, and you can't go to another god for another moral standard.

When anything else is worshiped, bad things result. Not only things that can obviously lead to evil such as the worship of power, or race, or money, or flag. But also things that are almost always seen as quite beautiful—such as art, or education, or even love. Yes, any of these often wonderful things, when worshiped, can lead to terrible results.

Take art. Many of the cruellest humans in history loved beautiful music and art. But, as a music lover, I learned early in life the sad fact that great music can be used to inspire people to follow evil just as much as it can be used to inspire people to do good. The great Hollywood director Stanley Kubrick vividly made this point in his classic 1971 film, *A Clockwork Orange.* In it, men rape and murder while classical music plays in the background.

Take education. We all recognize how important education can be—from preparing people to be able to find work to understanding the world. But education in and of itself, divorced from the higher ends of God and goodness, can lead, and often has led, to great evil. Many of the best-educated people in Germany supported Hitler and the Nazis. And almost all of the Western world's supporters of the genocidal regimes of Stalin in the Soviet Union and Mao in China were highly educated. There is nothing about a Ph.D. that guarantees a person will be wiser, kinder, or more ethical than someone with only a high school education.

The same holds true even of love. Love, of course, is so often beautiful. But it, too, can lead to evil. In the twentieth century people who put love of country above love of God and goodness often committed terrible evil.

And here's a test for you: Imagine that the pet you love and a stranger—a person you don't know and therefore could not possibly love—are drowning. Do you first try to save your pet or the stranger? Well, if love is an end in itself, you save your pet. But if you hold human life as a higher value than love, you won't follow love.

This commandment made the ethical revolution of the Bible and of the Ten Commandments—what is known as ethical monotheism—possible. Worship the God of the Ten Commandments and you will make a good world. Worship a false god—no matter how noble sounding—and you will end up with a world of cruelty.

STUDY QUESTIONS

1. Explain in your own words what the Second Commandment means.

2. What is the problem with thinking the Second Commandment only refers to ancient pagan gods?

3. What makes the Second Commandment the mother of all the other commandments?

4. How can the worship of education lead to having a negative impact on the world?

5. If a stranger and a pet you love are drowning and you save the pet, what does that mean? What does it mean if you save the stranger?

COMMANDMENT

DO NOT MISUSE
GOD'S NAME

THE WORST SIN YOU CAN COMMIT

s there such a thing as "the worst sin"—one sin that is worse than all others? Well, there is. I am well aware that some people differ. They maintain that we can't declare any sin worse than any other. "To God, a sin is a sin," is how it's often expressed. In this view, a person who steals a stapler from the office is committing as grievous a sin in God's eyes as a murderer. But most people intuitively, as well as biblically, understand that some sins are clearly worse than others. We are confident that God has at least as much common sense as we do. The God of Judaism and Christianity does not equate stealing an office item with murder.

So, then, what is the worst sin? The worst sin is committing evil in God's name. How do we know? From the

Third Commandment of the Ten Commandments. This is the only one of the Ten Commandments that states that God will not forgive a person who violates the commandment. What does this commandment say? It is most commonly translated as, "Do not take the name of the Lord thy God in vain. For the Lord will not hold guiltless"—meaning "will not forgive"—whoever takes His name in vain.

Most people understandably think that the commandment forbids saying God's name for no good reason. So, something like, "God, did I have a rough day at work today!" violates the Third Commandment. But that interpretation presents a real problem. It would mean that whereas God could forgive the violation of any of the other commandments—dishonoring one's parents, stealing, adultery, or even committing murder—He would never forgive someone who said, "God, did I have a rough day at work today!" Let's be honest: that would render

God and the Ten Commandments morally incomprehensible.

Well, as it happens, the commandment is not the problem. The problem is the translation. The Hebrew original doesn't say "Do not take"; it says "Do not carry." The Hebrew literally reads, "Do not carry the name of the Lord thy God in vain." One of the most widely used new translations of the Bible, the New International Version, or NIV, uses the word "misuse" rather than the word "take": "You shall not misuse the name of the Lord your God." This is much closer to the original's intent.

What does it mean to "carry" or to "misuse" God's name? It means committing evil in God's name. And that God will not forgive. Why not? When an irreligious person commits evil, it doesn't bring God and religion into disrepute. But when religious people commit evil, especially in God's name, they are not only committing evil, they are doing terrible damage to the name of God.

In our time, there is an example of this. The evils committed by Islamists who torture, bomb, cut throats, and mass murder—all in the name of God—do terrible damage to the name of God. It is not coincidental that what is called the New Atheism—the immense eruption of atheist activism—followed the 9/11 attacks on America by Islamist terrorists. In fact, the most frequent argument against God and religion concerns evil committed in God's name—whether it is done in the name of Allah today or was done in the past in the name of Christ.

People who murder in the name of God not only kill their victims, they kill God, too. That's why the greatest sin is religious evil. That's what the Third Commandment is there to teach: don't carry God's name in vain. If you do, God won't forgive you.

STUDY QUESTIONS

1. Explain in your own words what the Third Commandment means.

2. What is different about this commandment from all the others?

3. How does the original Hebrew differ from many English translations? What translation more matches the intent of the original language?

4. How is this commandment commonly misinterpreted?

5. Provide an example of what it means to break the Third Commandment.

COMMANDMENT

IV

REMEMBER THE SABBATH DAY

DON'T BE A SLAVE

Many people who revere the Ten Commandments don't think that the Fourth is particularly important, let alone binding. Once you understand it, however, you will recognize how life-changing, even world-changing, the Sabbath commandment is. And you will begin to appreciate how relevant it is to your own life.

The Fourth Commandment reads: "Remember the Sabbath Day to keep it holy. Six days you shall labor and do all your work, but the seventh day is a Sabbath to the Lord your God. On it you shall not do any work, neither you, nor your son nor daughter, nor your male or female servant, nor your animals, nor any foreigner residing in your towns."

Why is this so important?

First, perhaps more than any other commandment, it elevated the human being. How so? For nearly all of human history, life consisted overwhelmingly of work. In effect, humans were beasts of burden. This commandment and only this commandment changed all that by insisting that people cease working one day out of seven.

Second, more than any other commandment, the Sabbath Day reminds people that they are meant to be free. As the second version of the Commandment—the one summarized by Moses in the Book of Deuteronomy—states, "Remember that you were slaves in Egypt." In other words, remember that slaves cannot have a Sabbath. In light of this, I might add that in the biblical view, unless necessary for survival, people who choose to work seven days a week are essentially slaves—slaves to work or perhaps to money, but slaves nonetheless. The millionaire who works seven days a week is simply a rich slave.

Third, while the Bible could not universally abolish slavery, the Sabbath commandment greatly humanized that terrible institution and even helped make slavery impossible. By definition, a slave owner was under no obligation to allow a slave to ever rest, let alone to rest one day every week. Yet, that is exactly what the Fourth Commandment commanded. Even a slave has fundamental human rights. Therefore a slave too, is a human being.

Fourth, the Sabbath almost singlehandedly creates and strengthens family ties and friendships. When a person takes off from work one day every week, that day almost inevitably becomes a day spent with other people—namely, family and/or friends. It has similar positive effects on marriages. Ask anyone married to a workaholic how good it would be for their marriage if the workaholic would not work for one day each week—and you can appreciate the power of the Sabbath Day.

Fifth, the Sabbath commandment granted animals dignity. Even one's animals had to rest one day a week. It is, to the best of our knowledge, the first national law in history on behalf of animals. And its benefits to animals surely went beyond a mandatory day of rest for them. People who felt divinely obligated to give their animals a day of rest were much less likely to treat their animals cruelly any day of the week.

Now, all five of these life-changing and society-changing benefits of the Sabbath are available to anyone. You don't have to be a Jew, a Christian, or even a believer in God to derive all these benefits. But the reality is that those who believe the Ten Commandments were given by God are the ones who have kept the Sabbath alive.

The God factor plays another role in the Sabbath. Just as faith in God brings people to the Sabbath, observing the Sabbath brings people to faith in God. That is why the first version of the Ten Commandments, the version in the Book of Exodus, ends with these words: "For in six days God made the heavens and the earth, the sea, and all that is in them, but he rested on the seventh day. Therefore God blessed the Sabbath day and made it holy."

However you interpret six days, the point is this. Every time you keep the Sabbath you are affirming that there is a Creator, that the world didn't just happen, that life isn't some meaningless coincidence, but that it is infinitely meaningful and therefore each of us has a unique significance and purpose.

Not bad for one day a week. No wonder that the Sabbath is one of the Ten Commandments. No wonder that those who have it in their lives are often happier, with richer family lives, more serenity, a community of friends, and, yes, are even healthier. You might want to give it a try.

STUDY QUESTIONS

1. Explain in your own words what the Fourth Commandment means.

2. How did this commandment elevate the human being?

3. What effect did this commandment have on slavery?

4. What does it mean if you're a millionaire who works seven days a week?

5. What are some of the effects on a person's life when this commandment is observed?

COMMANDMENT

V

HONOR YOUR FATHER AND MOTHER

EVEN IF YOU DON'T FEEL LIKE IT

The Fifth of the Ten Commandments reads: "Honor your father and your mother."

This commandment is so important that it is one of the only commandments in the entire Bible that gives a reason for observing it: "That your days may be long in the land that the LORD your God is giving you."

Many people read that part of the Fifth Commandment as a reward. But while it may be regarded as a reward, the fact remains that it is a reason: if you build a society in which children honor their parents, your society will long survive. And the corollary is: a society in which children do not honor their parents is doomed to self-destruction.

In our time, this connection between honoring parents and maintaining civilization is not widely recognized. On the contrary, many of the best-educated parents do not believe that their children need to show them honor, since "honoring" implies an authority figure, and that is a status many modern parents reject. In addition, many parents seek to be loved, not honored, by their children. Yet, neither the Ten Commandments nor the Bible elsewhere commands us to love our parents. This is particularly striking given that the Bible commands us to love our neighbor, to love God, and to love the stranger.

The Bible understands that there will always be individuals who, for whatever reason, do not love a parent. Therefore, it does not demand what may be psychologically or emotionally impossible. But it does demand that we show honor to our parents. And it makes this demand only with regard to parents. There is no one else whom the Bible commands us to honor.

So, then, why is honoring parents so important? Why do the Ten Commandments believe that society could not survive if this commandment were widely violated? One reason is that we, as children, need it. Parents may *want* to be honored—and they should want to be—but children *need* to honor parents. A father and a mother who are not honored are essentially adult peers of their children. They are not parents. No generation knows better than ours the terrible consequences of growing up without a father. Fatherless boys are far more likely to grow up and commit violent crime, mistreat women, and act out against society in every other way. Girls who do not have a father to honor—and, hopefully, to love as well—are more likely to seek the wrong men and to be promiscuous at an early age.

Second, honoring parents is how nearly all of us come to recognize that there is a moral authority above us to whom we are morally accountable. And without this, we cannot create or maintain a moral society. Of course, for the Ten Commandments, the ultimate moral authority is God, Who is therefore higher than even our parents. But it is very difficult to come to honor God without having had a parent, especially a father, to honor. Sigmund Freud, the father of psychiatry and an atheist, theorized that one's attitude toward one's father largely shaped one's attitude toward God.

There is one more reason why honoring parents is fundamental to a good society. Honoring parents is the best antidote to totalitarianism. One of the first things totalitarian movements seek to do is to break the child-parent bond. The child's allegiance is shifted from parents to the state. Even in democratic societies the larger the state becomes, the more it usurps the parental role.

Finally, there are many ways to honor parents. The general rule is this: they get special treatment. Parents are unique; so they must be treated in a unique way. You don't talk to them in quite the same way you do anyone else. For example, you might use expletives when speaking to a friend, but you don't with a parent. You don't call them by their first name. And when you leave their home and make your own, you maintain contact with them. Having no contact with parents is the opposite of honoring them.

And, yes, we all recognize that some parents have behaved so cruelly—and I mean cruelly, not annoyingly—that one finds it morally impossible to honor them. There are such cases. But they are rare.

And remember this, if your children see you honor your parents, no matter how difficult it may sometimes be, the chances are far greater that they will honor you.

STUDY QUESTIONS

1. Explain in your own words what the Fifth
    Commandment means.

2. Do children need to honor their parents? Why
    or why not?

3. How is honoring parents the best antidote to
    totalitarianism?

4. Why does the Bible command us to honor our
    parents and not love them?

5. Give two examples of ways parents can be
    honored.

COMMANDMENT

VI

DO NOT MURDER

YOU CAN KILL, BUT YOU
CAN'T MURDER

You would think that of all the Ten Commandments the one that needs the least
explaining is the Sixth, because it seems so
clear. It is the one that the King James Bible, the most
widely used English translation of the Bible, translates
as "Thou shall not kill." Yet, the truth is quite the opposite. This is probably the least well understood of the
Ten Commandments.

The reason is that the Hebrew original does not say,
"Do not kill." It says, "Do not murder." Both Hebrew
and English have two words for taking a life—one is
"kill" (*harag*, הרג, in Hebrew) and the other is "murder"
(*ratsach*, רצח, in Hebrew).

The difference between the two is enormous. Kill means:

1. Taking any life—whether of a human being or an animal.

2. Taking a human life deliberately or by accident.

3. Taking a human life legally or illegally, morally or immorally.

On the other hand, murder can only mean one thing:

The illegal or immoral taking of a human life.

That's why we say, "I killed a mosquito," not "I murdered a mosquito."

And that's why we would say, "The worker was accidentally killed," not "The worker was accidentally murdered."

So why did the King James translation of the Bible use the word "kill" rather than "murder"? Because four hundred years ago when the translation was made, "kill" was synonymous with "murder." As a result, some people don't realize that English has changed since 1610 and therefore think that the Ten Commandments prohibit all killing. But, of course, they don't. If the Ten Commandments forbade killing, we would all have to be vegetarians—killing animals would be prohibited. And we would all have to be pacifists—since we could not kill even in self-defense.

However, you don't have to know how the English language has evolved in order to understand that the Ten Commandments could not have prohibited all killing. The very same part of the Bible that contains the Ten Commandments—the Five Books of Moses, the

Torah as it is known by Jews—commands the death penalty for murder, allows killing in war, prescribes animal sacrifice, and allows eating meat.

A correct understanding of the commandment against murder is crucial because, while virtually every modern translation correctly translates the commandment as "Do not murder," many people cite the King James translation to justify two positions that have no biblical basis: opposition to capital punishment and pacifism.

Regarding capital punishment and the Bible, the only law that appears in each one of the Five Books of Moses is that murderers be put to death. Opponents of the death penalty are free to hold the view that all murderers should be allowed to live. But they are not free to cite the Bible to support their view. Yet, many do.

And they always cite the commandment, "Do not kill." But that, as should now be abundantly clear, is not what the commandment says, and it is therefore an invalid argument.

As regards pacifism, the belief that it is always wrong to kill a human being, again, anyone is free to hold this position, as immoral as it may be. And what other word than "immoral" can one use to describe forbidding the killing of someone who is in the process of murdering innocent men, women, and children, in, let's say, a movie theater or a school?

But it is dishonest to cite the commandment against murder to justify pacifism. There is moral killing—most obviously when done in self-defense against an aggressor—and there is immoral killing. And the word for that is murder.

The Ten Commandments are portrayed on two tablets. The five commandments on the second tablet all concern our treatment of fellow human beings.

The first one on that list is "Do not murder." Why? Because murder is the worst act a person can commit. The other four commandments—prohibiting stealing, adultery, giving false testimony, and coveting, are all serious offenses. But murder leads the list because deliberately taking the life of an innocent person is the most terrible thing we can do.

The next time you hear someone cite "Do not kill" when quoting the Sixth Commandment, gently but firmly explain that it actually says "Do not murder."

STUDY QUESTIONS

1. Explain in your own words what the Sixth Commandment means.

2. Why is this the least well-understood commandment?

3. What is the difference between "killing" and "murdering"?

4. How do opponents of the death penalty use the Bible to support their position? Is this argument valid or invalid? Why?

5. Can the Sixth Commandment be used to justify pacifism? Why or why not?

COMMANDMENT

VII

DO NOT COMMIT ADULTERY

THE BEST WAY TO PROTECT
THE FAMILY

There is an old joke about the Seventh Commandment, "Do Not Commit Adultery." Moses comes down from Mount Sinai, and announces: "I have good news and bad news. The good news is that I got Him down to ten. The bad news is that adultery stays."

The joke is telling. The prohibition on a married person having sexual relations with anyone except his or her spouse may be, for many people, the most consistently difficult of the Ten Commandments to observe. The reasons shouldn't be hard to guess.

One is the enormous power of the sex drive. It can be very hard to keep in check for the entirety of one's marriage—especially when an attractive outsider makes him or herself sexually or romantically available. Another reason is the human desire to love and be loved. For normal people, there is no more powerful emotion than love. If one falls in love with someone while married, it takes great effort not to commit adultery with that person. And if we add in the unfortunate circumstance of a loveless marriage, adultery becomes even more difficult to resist. That's why the joke with which I began is funny—because it reflects truth.

Why is adultery prohibited in the Ten Commandments? Because, like the other nine, it is indispensable to forming and maintaining higher civilization. Adultery threatens the very building block of the civilization that the Ten Commandments seek to create. That building block is the family—a married father and mother and their children. Anything that threatens the family unit is prohibited in the Bible. Adultery is one example. Not honoring one's father and mother is another. And the prohibition on injecting any sexuality into the family unit—incest—is a third example.

Why is the family so important? Because without it, social stability is impossible. Because without it, the passing on of society's values from generation to generation is impossible. Because commitment to a wife and children makes men more responsible and mature. Because, more than anything else, family meets most women's deepest emotional and material needs. And nothing comes close to the family in giving children a secure and stable childhood.

And why does adultery threaten the family? The most obvious reason is that sex with someone other than one's spouse can all too easily lead to either or both spouses leaving the marriage. Adultery should not automatically lead to divorce, but it often does.

There is another reason adultery can destroy a family. It can lead to pregnancy and then to the birth of a child. That child will in almost all cases start out life with no family—meaning no father and mother married to each other—to call his or her own.

And if adultery doesn't destroy a family, it almost always does terrible harm to a marriage. Aside from the sense of betrayal and loss of trust that it causes, it means that the adulterous partner lives a fraudulent life. When a husband or wife is having sex with someone other than their spouse, their thoughts are constantly about that other person and about how to deceive their spouse. The life of deception that an adulterous affair necessarily entails inevitably damages a marriage even if the betrayed spouse is unaware of the affair.

Finally, the commandment prohibiting adultery doesn't come with an asterisk saying that adultery is okay if both spouses agree to it. Spouses who have extramarital sex with the permission of their husband or wife may not hurt their spouse's feelings, but they are still harming the institution of marriage. And protecting the family, not protecting spouses from emotional pain, is the reason for the commandment.

Many marriages, sadly, are troubled. And it is not for any of us to stand in judgment of others' behavior in this realm. No one knows what goes on in anyone else's marriage. And if we did, we might often well understand why one or the other sought love outside the marriage. But no higher civilization can be made or can endure that condones adultery. That is why it is prohibited in the Ten Commandments.

STUDY QUESTIONS

1. Explain in your own words what the Seventh Commandment means.

2. What is the main reason for the Seventh Commandment?

3. How does breaking the Seventh Commandment threaten social stability?

4. Give one example of how adultery negatively affects the family unit.

5. Is there a situation in which committing adultery is not considered wrong? Why or why not?

COMMANDMENT

VIII

DO NOT STEAL

KEEP THIS AND YOU'LL
KEEP THEM ALL

A good case can be made that the Eighth Commandment, "Do Not Steal," is the one commandment that encompasses all the others.

How does "Do not Steal" encompass the other commandments? Murder is the stealing of another person's life. Adultery is the stealing of another person's spouse. Coveting is the desire to steal what belongs to another person. Giving false testimony is stealing justice. And so on.

This commandment is unique in another way: it is the only commandment that is completely open-ended. All the other commandments are specific. The Fifth Commandment, for example, states that it is our parents whom we should honor. The Sixth Commandment, prohibiting murder, is about taking the life of an innocent human being. The Seventh Commandment, prohibiting adultery, is also specific—to a married person. Two unmarried people cannot commit adultery. But the commandment against stealing doesn't even hint at what it is we are forbidden to steal. Which means that we cannot take anything that belongs to another person. And that, in turn, means three big things.

First and foremost, the commandment against stealing has always been understood to mean that we are not allowed to steal another human being—what we call kidnapping. That is why no one who had even an elementary understanding of the Eighth Commandment could ever use the Bible to justify the most common form of slavery—the kidnapping of human beings and selling them into slavery. Critics of the Bible argue that the Bible allowed slavery. But the type of slavery described was in almost all cases what was known as indentured servitude, the selling of oneself to another person for a fixed period of time in order to work off a debt. This had nothing to do with kidnapping free people—such as was done in Africa and elsewhere. That was expressly forbidden by the Eighth Commandment.

The second significant meaning of the commandment against stealing is the sanctity of people's property. Just as we are forbidden to steal people, we are forbidden to steal what people own. It has been shown over and over that private property, beginning with land ownership, is indispensable to creating a free and decent society. Every totalitarian regime takes away private property rights. In the ancient and medieval world a few rich people owned all the land and the majority of the population worked on that land for the enrichment of the owners. And then, in nineteenth century Europe, many socialists argued for taking away private property and giving it to the "people." Where that advice was followed, in what came to be known as the communist world, theft of property quickly resulted in theft of freedom, and ultimately massive theft of life.

The third enormously important meaning of the commandment against stealing concerns the many non-material things each person owns: their reputation, their dignity, their trust, and their intellectual property. Let's quickly run through these.

1. A person's reputation. Stealing a person's good name—whether through libel, slander, or gossip—is a particularly destructive form of theft. Because, unlike

money or property, once a person's good name has been stolen, it can almost never be fully restored.

2. A person's dignity. The act of stealing a person's dignity is known as humiliation. And humiliating a person, especially in public, can do permanent damage to what is perhaps the most precious thing any of us owns—our dignity.

3. A person's trust. Stealing a person's trust is known as deceiving someone. In fact, in Hebrew a term for tricking someone is *g'neivat da'at* (גניבת דעת), which literally means "stealing knowledge." One example is tricking people into buying something, as when a real estate agent omits telling a prospective purchaser all the flaws in a home, in order to make a sale. Another example would be when someone

deceives another person with insincere proclamations of love in order to obtain material or sexual favors.

4. A person's intellectual property. This form of theft includes anything from copying software or downloading music and movies without paying for them to stealing a person's words, what we know as plagiarism.

Stealing a life, a person, a spouse, material property, intellectual property, a reputation, dignity, or trust: there is hardly any aspect of human life that is not harmed—sometimes irreparably so—by stealing. That is why it is fair to say that if everyone observed only one of the Ten Commandments, observing the commandment "Do Not Steal" would, all by itself, make a beautiful world.

STUDY QUESTIONS

1. Explain in your own words what the Eighth Commandment means.

2. Does the Bible justify slavery? Why or why not?

3. What unique quality does the Eighth Commandment have?

4. Explain how the Eight Commandment encompasses all of the other commandments.

5. Give three examples of non-material things that a person can steal.

COMMANDMENT

IX

DO NOT
BEAR FALSE
WITNESS

LYING IS THE ROOT OF EVIL

The Ninth of the Ten Commandments is "You shall not give false witness against your neighbor." This means two things: "Do not lie when testifying in court." And, "Do not lie." Period. Remember, in order for an action to be prohibited or demanded in the Ten Commandments it has to be fundamental to making civilization. As important as donkey riding might have been when the Ten Commandments were given, the Ten Commandments contain no commandment to ride your donkey responsibly. A society can survive bad donkey drivers. But it cannot survive contempt for truth—whether inside or outside a courtroom. If people testify falsely in a courtroom, there can be no justice. And without even the hope of justice, there can be no civilization.

The Hebrew Bible was so adamant on this subject that the punishment imposed on a witness who gave false testimony was the same as the punishment that would have been meted out to the accused had the false testimony been believed. In the case of a crime that would be punishable by death, therefore, the false witness was liable to be put to death. But the commandment is clearly concerned with truth generally, not only in a courtroom.

Both the great twelfth century Jewish commentator, Abraham Ibn Ezra, and one of the most influential biblical scholars of the twentieth century, Brevard Childs of Yale University, agreed that the commandment was about truth-telling generally. As Childs pointed out, if the Ten Commandments were solely concerned with truth and falsehood in a courtroom, they would have added words such as "in court."

There are many important values in society, but truth is probably the most important. Goodness and compassion may be the most important values in the micro, or personal, realm. But in the macro, or societal, realm, truth is even more important than compassion or kindness. Virtually all the great societal evils, such as African slavery, Nazism, and Communism, have been based on lies.

There were slave traders, Nazis, and Communists who were compassionate in their personal lives, but all of them told, and most of them believed, some great lie that enabled them to participate in a great evil. Black slavery was made possible in large measure by the lie that blacks were innately inferior to whites. The Holocaust would have been impossible without tens of millions of people believing the lie that Jews were inherently inferior to so-called Aryans. And Communist totalitarianism was entirely based on lies. That's why the Soviet Union's Communist Party newspaper was named *Pravda*, the Russian word for "Truth"—because the Party, not objective reality, was the source of truth.

There is only so much evil that can be done by individual sadists and sociopaths. In order to murder millions, vast numbers of otherwise normal, even decent, people must believe lies. Mass evil is committed not because a vast number of people seek to be cruel, but because they are fed lies that convince them that what is evil is actually good. However, one big obstacle to truth-telling is that believers in causes, including good causes, that don't place truth as a central value, will be very tempted to lie on behalf of their cause.

There are many examples. In the 1980s, to promote the cause of the homeless, the leading activist on their behalf claimed that there were 2 to 3 million homeless in the United States. Years later he admitted on national television that he had to come up with a number and made that one up. The real number was between 250,000 and 350,000.

Similarly, groups in the fight against cancer were caught greatly exaggerating the number of women who get breast cancer each year. Why? In order to frighten more women into getting mammograms. Again, lying on behalf of a good cause. Why is lying on behalf of good causes destructive? Because if we don't know what's true, how and where do we know how to properly allocate society's limited resources? And in the worst cases, it distorts society's priorities, and therefore does great harm.

The Ten Commandments are there to warn all of us that, with very few exceptions, such as the immediate saving of innocent life, no cause is more important than truth-telling. The Ten Commandments are the greatest list of instructions ever devised for creating a good society. But such a society cannot be created or maintained if it is not based on truth.

STUDY QUESTIONS

1. Explain in your own words what the Ninth Commandment means.

2. What example from the Hebrew Bible shows how important truth is?

3. What is the most important value in society? Why?

4. What must happen in order for mass evil to happen in the world?

5. Why is lying on behalf of good causes wrong?

COMMANDMENT

DO NOT COVET

THE ONE THOUGHT YOU
SHOULD NEVER HAVE

I n the Ten Commandments, Commandments Six, Seven, Eight, and Nine are the ones that prohibit acts of evil—murder, adultery, stealing, and perjury. And then there is one commandment that prohibits the thing that leads to murder, adultery, stealing, and perjury. Which one is it? It's the last of the Ten: do not covet anything that belongs to others—not their spouse, their house, their servants, their animals, or any of their property.

In order to understand this commandment, and its unique significance, the first thing to understand is that this is the only one of the Ten Commandments that legislates thought. All the other commandments legislate behavior. In fact, of the 613 laws in the Five Books of Moses, virtually none prohibit thought.

Why, then, do the Ten Commandments include a law that prohibits a thought? Because it is coveting that so often leads to evil. Or, to put it another way, coveting is what leads to violating the preceding four commandments—the ones against murder, adultery, stealing, and perjury. Think about it. Why do people do those things? In most instances, it is because they covet something that belongs to another person. Obviously that is the reason people steal—thieves covet their victims' property. But it is also the reason for many murders. And coveting is obviously the reason for adultery—wanting the spouse of another person. As for perjury—or "bearing false witness" in the language of the Ten Commandments—that is done in order to cover up all these other crimes that are caused by coveting.

But in order to understand why coveting is the one thought that is prohibited in the Ten Commandments and one of the only thoughts prohibited in the entire Hebrew Bible, we need to understand what coveting means—and, equally important, what it doesn't mean.

To covet is much more than "to want." The Hebrew verb, *lachmod* (לחמוד), means to want to the point of seeking to take away and own something that belongs to another person. Note that there are two operative elements here: "seeking to own," and "belongs to another person." "Seeking to own" does not mean just envying or, in the case of your neighbor's spouse, just lusting after. Neither envy nor lust is prohibited in the Ten Commandments. Uncontrolled envy and lust can surely lead to bad things, and they can both be psychologically and emotionally destructive, but neither one is prohibited in the Ten Commandments. Why? Because neither is the same as coveting. It is coveting that almost inevitably leads to stealing, to adultery, and sometimes even to murder.

Let me explain this in another way. The Tenth Commandment does not prohibit you from saying, "Wow, what a great house (or car or spouse) my neighbor has. I wish I had such a house (or car or spouse)." That may end up being destructive. But it may also end up being constructive. How? It may spur you to work harder and improve your life so that you can obtain a house, car, or spouse like your neighbor's. It is when you want—and seek to gain possession of—the specific house, car, or spouse that belongs to another that evil ensues. And that is what the Tenth Commandment prohibits.

Therefore one of these Ten Commandments, these ten basic rules of life, must be that we simply cannot allow ourselves to covet what belongs to our neighbor. Whatever belongs to another person must be regarded as sacrosanct. We cannot seek to own anything that belongs to another. Because only evil can come of it.

STUDY QUESTIONS

1. Explain in your own words what the Tenth Commandment means.

2. How is this commandment related to the preceding four commandments?

3. What does coveting mean and what does it not mean?

4. How are envy and lust different from coveting?

5. Is saying, "Wow, what a great car my neighbor has. I wish I had such a car," considered coveting? Why or why not?